Personal Growth and Development

CREATIVE
VISUALIZATION

MONIQUE JOINER SIEDLAK

Oshun
Publications

Cover Design by MJS

Cover Image by agsandrew and nordenworks @depositphotos.com

Published by Oshun Publications

www.oshunpublications.com

Contents

Books in the Series

Personal and Self Development
Astral Projection for Beginners
Meditation for Beginners
Reiki for Beginners
Manifesting With the Law of Attraction
Stress Management
Time Bound: Setting Your Goals
Healing Animals with Reiki

Want to learn about African Magic, Wicca, or even Reiki while cleaning your home, exercising, or driving to work? I know it's tough these days to simply find the time to relax and curl up with a good book. This is why I'm delighted to share that I have books available in audiobook format.

Best of all, you can get the audiobook version of this book or any other book by me for free as part of a 30-day Audible trial.

Members get free audiobooks every month and exclusive discounts. It's an excellent way to explore and determine if audiobook learning works for you.

If you're not satisfied, you can cancel anytime within the

trial period. You won't be charged, and you can still keep your book. To choose your free audiobook, visit:

www.mojosiedlak.com/free-audiobooks

WANT TO BE FIRST TO KNOW?!

JOIN MY NEWSLETTER!
MOJOSIEDLAK.COM/SELF-HELP-AND-YOGA-NEWSLETTER

Introduction

We have far more control over our lives than we give ourselves credit for.

It is common for people to feel that they have no control over their lives or their futures. They may have goals and ideas of what they want to do, but they think it is beyond their control. However, if you start off thinking that something is unattainable, you have already lost. You have already admitted defeat if you cannot conceive a possible future to achieve what you want.

This moment is where creative visualization comes in.

Creative visualization is a mindfulness technique that allows you to envision your goals and subsequently achieve them. It is the idea that the only way to truly succeed is to see yourself growing, fully believing that the future you can imagine is possible.

Why not imagine we have two friends going to a party tonight: the one friend believes he will have the best time. He can see himself showing up and being the life of the party— talking to everyone and meeting a ton of new and exciting people. The other friend is a bit more nervous, though: he does not tend to do well with parties and meeting new people.

When he thinks ahead to the party, he sees himself either following around his friend—because that would be the only person he knows—or sitting and drinking in the kitchen by himself. Who do you think is going to have a better time at the party?

By focusing on the worst possible outcome, the second friend is willing that future into existence. He is going into a situation with a preexisting negative view of what is going to happen. Because of this, he is more likely to act in accordance with that vision. He will not try and be outgoing or talk to new people because he cannot conceive a future where that would go well. Unfortunately, his biggest problem had begun far before the event arrived.

Creative visualization is essentially using your imagination to create and guide your life. It is about conjuring up images of how you want your life to look, believing in them so wholeheartedly that they will become a reality. This ideal is something everyone already does unconsciously, though not as mindfully as we could. We are continually looking ahead and imagining in our heads how things are going to go. Often though, we do this absently. Or perhaps, we are more prone to looking at the worst-case scenario. Creative visualization is about taking this habit and doing it more mindfully and purposely. It is about harnessing the giant well of untapped potential: our mind and our imagination.

By learning to visualize and manifest what we want in life, we naturally attract those possibilities to us. We gain the confidence to believe we can do anything and attract people to help us achieve these things. By learning to control and harness your imagination, creative visualization allows you to do anything you set your mind to do.

ONE

What Is Creative Visualization?

THE CONCEPT OF CREATIVE VISUALIZATION IS NOT ONE THAT IS relatively new to humanity. As an intentional practice, the theory is that it has been around for centuries. The concept of 'the mind's eye' was developed by the Roman statesman, Cicero, in Ancient Rome. This concept was the idea that a specific part of your consciousness dealt with creating images. The same view was present in Geoffrey Chaucer's Canterbury Tales (Harell, 2018). The definition of a 'mind's eye' is a cognitive process of deliberating and creating mental images to stimulate the subconscious, transforming those images into reality (Gawain, 1995). It is also about using your natural imagination and abilities to change emotions or feelings typically associated with a particular situation, resulting in significant physical, emotional, or psychological change.

The most crucial part about practicing creative visualization is that the scenarios or futures you imagine must feel real to you. It should never feel like a daydream—it must feel like a close reality. For example, imagine that you are unhappy in your current job and want to start looking for a new one. You will sit down and visualize the working environment you want. The kind of people you want to work with, and all the minute details of what exactly you are looking for in that career. The more you pin down the details, the more real your visualization will feel. It will only become a reality if you already perceive it to be one.

Furthermore, creative visualization intends never to change other people or control their behaviors but instead change us. Gawain (1995) states, "Its effect is to dissolve our internal barriers to natural harmony and self-realization, allowing everyone to manifest in his or her most positive aspect." Creative visualization is about changing your own behaviors to create change. This idea is not surface level; you are not trying to merely adopt a positive attitude. It is about fundamentally changing your "deepest, most basic attitudes towards life" (Ashokananda, 2015).

The practice of creative visualization involves finding a quiet space during a time of day when you feel you are the calmest and most centered with your mind and body. Choose a goal—something that you want to achieve either personally or professionally. You can decide that you want to visualize getting a new job or meeting someone new. Close your eyes and breath deeply for a few minutes; soon after this, begin to imagine the goal you want to achieve. Visualize yourself meeting someone new and going on a date. Take your time to add in more and more details until the vision starts to feel real —this is creative visualization.

Furthermore, practicing visualization is something that we all do every single day, though we do it in little actions. Every original action comes from an idea. It comes from you deciding on a future that you want. This could be in the simple things you do every day.: for example, when you feel hungry and decide what you will eat for dinner. You think about what you will have, and then you envision the dish you have decided on in your head. This is creative visualization, though in a smaller and less deliberate form.

The mindful practice of creative visualization aims to take this subconscious practice and use it for its full potential.

Central Principles of Creative Visualization

The building of creative visualization happens with several different principles. First and foremost, the ideology bases on the fact that we have far more power over our minds and actions than we realize. We often attribute changes in our lives to our thoughts and not our actions. However, all actions—conscious or subconscious—stem from our thoughts. We have to make decisions before we act. Even the basis of our most unconscious decisions happen with thoughts and feelings we have already made. For example, suppose we have decided our whole life that we do not like broccoli when we choose to have supper. In that case, we will now choose to avoid broccoli at all costs—this happens whether we think about it consciously or not. A central principle of creative visualization is noticing these subconscious feelings or decisions and rewiring the ones that are harmful to us. Another way would be merely creating new choices that will have a positive impact on our lives. It is about taking control of your thoughts and making a conscious effort to rewire how you think.

This idea of rewiring your outlook links to one of the other central principles of creative visualization: positivity. Suppose your default outlook on life is one of negativity. In that case, you are going to struggle to envision and truly accept situations that involve you leading your best possible life. If you naturally look towards the worst-case scenario, that is what you will visualize. Your attempt at creative visualization will fail. This mentality is why one of the pillars of creative visualization is reworking your gut reaction to positivity.

It is also essential to understand that creative visualization is not a fast solution to all the problems you may be experiencing in life. It is not a technique that you practice for a week and then suddenly find yourself living the life you have always dreamed about. If you want success, you still have to work for it (Denning & Phillips, 1981). If you want a more comfortable lifestyle, for example, you still have to put in the hours and the hard work to get the money and make it happen. Creative visualization does not do it for you—it merely shows you that you are capable.

Additionally, creative visualization helps you subconsciously change your actions, so you are working towards that lifestyle. It helps you attract people with similar energies and goals that will help you.; it gives you all the tools you need to accomplish your goals.

Lastly, creative visualization should start as a mindful practice and eventually become a habit. When you start practicing creative visualization, it is crucial to begin with a specific goal in mind. This can be anything from finding a new job or making some new friends. Starting with smaller and more specific goals allows you to practice creative visualization and be more focused on mastering it. However, your ultimate goal should be to use creative visualization as a reflex in every aspect of your life. After you start practicing, it should become a habit that helps you achieve all of your goals; it should be something that you begin to do before you even realize it. By doing this, you will find success and happiness in all spheres of your life.

TWO

Why Creative Visualization Works
_____

CREATIVE VISUALIZATION IS USEFUL BECAUSE IT "INVOLVES
understanding and aligning yourself with the natural principles that govern the working of our universe" (Gawain, 1995).
You are aligning your three different worlds and aligning this
inner self with the world around you. By reworking your
subconscious, you can affect
     your mind's other levels. Ultimately changing your gut
instincts and the way you act without consciously being aware
of it.
     Creative visualization primarily works because it rewires
the way you think. If you imagine your mind as software—by
changing your beliefs and how you view things—you are
changing your programming (Brenner, 2016). If you program
your mind to make decisions that lead to something you may
want, you will always succeed. Because creative visualization
works through all the levels of your subconscious, the so-called
programming is more effective. Below, we will start to look at
the different layers that comprise your inner self and how they
work together to make creative visualization effective.

Our Three Worlds

Understanding our connection to the world around us—our environment—is essential to understanding how visualization works. Our three worlds—or more commonly known as the three worlds of existence in Buddhism—explains the "existence of individual lives in the real world" and how our consciousness fits in with the world around us (Gakkai, 2020).

The first world that we experience is the five components' realm: this is how we interact with and interpret our surroundings. The five elements we use are form, perception, conception, volition, and consciousness (Gakkai, 2020); this world is internal and unique to each individual. Form refers to our body and how we present ourselves. Perception is how we perceive the world; conception is how we process that information. Volition is the will to do something with the information we collect. Lastly—and most importantly—consciousness is how we integrate the four other components. Our consciousness is key to creative visualization because it contains all of the other four worlds.

The second world that we have is the realm of living beings. This world refers to the individual composed of the five realms within them—the one who "manifest experiences." It also refers to how these individuals interact with one another (Gakkai, 2020).

The third and final world is the realm of the environment. This is "the place or land where living beings dwell and carry out life-activities" (Gakkai, 2020). The state of the environment is dependent on how living beings treat it.

Creative visualization is powerful because it links all three of our worlds and uses one to influence the other. By influencing the five components' realm, we can change how we perceive and interact with the world around us. For creative visualization to work, one needs to understand how we fit into the world around us, and how changing something about ourselves echoes throughout our three worlds.

The Mind

Our mind is not as far beyond our control as we think. While we tend to think of our mind as something that controls us, we are in charge of the entire thing in reality. It functions just like any other muscle in the body, so training the mind is vital to fully utilizing it. Creative visualization is about learning to use your mind to its full potential; it is about exercising the muscle until it is strong. You can use it to influence the world around you.

The mind splits into two parts: the conscious mind and the subconscious mind. They are interconnected—the subconscious mind relies on the conscious mind for information from the external world. The conscious mind depends on the subconscious mind for internal communication. For visualization to be effective, one has to utilize this connection.

The Conscious Mind

Our conscious mind is where we have the most control; therefore, most of the creative visualization work will occur. This is the level of your mind that you are entirely aware of. It is the voice you hear in your head, and how you make decisions you are aware of making. We also use it to process the world around us and make use of it to "take in input from our senses, analyze the information, and then make decisions based on this information" (Ramsay, 2019).

This section is the part of the mind that we use to visualize. Although we are ultimately trying to reprogram your subconscious mind, the conscious mind is where we envision the images and scenarios to do that.

The Subconscious Mind

Our subconscious mind is the part of our mind that influences every thought, feeling, and action we have without fully comprehending it. The subconscious is the part of your mind that does the mindless things for you. It is deep inside us and proves almost unreachable (Webster, 2006). It makes up roughly 90% of our brain and is mostly unused. The subconscious is the part of our mind that creates our experience and determines how we interpret and view the world.

Additionally, the subconscious never happens by reality but is influenced by what we experience and perceive. Therefore, if one practices creative visualization consistently, those images' repetition causes the subconscious to accept them as reality. Furthermore, by repeating the visualization of these actions or scenarios, they become like second nature to us. Thus, when we actually perform the behavior, it comes naturally to us because it has been ingrained in our neural pathways. (Mueller, 2016). The key to truly changing the subconscious is through images, feelings, and experiences. Therefore, using creative visualization to generate those is highly effective in convincing your subconscious of a new reality.

Creative visualization is powerful because it relies on our mind: our mind is the most powerful thing we have at our disposal. By visualizing every day and internalizing ideas as reality, we can shape our subconscious. Because our future goals are now real to our subconscious, we begin to act accordingly without our conscious knowledge. We will make decisions based on this new information, which will ultimately lead us to our goal. Visualization works because it uses our subconscious's power—which is mainly unused—and taps into that unlimited potential.

THREE

The Power of Creative Visualization
_____

As children, we are told not to daydream; in fact, we get punished for losing focus and slipping into our imagination as soon as we enter school. From that point on, we, unfortunately, use our imagination less and less. We are taught to use formulas and follow the rules, forgetting the silly daydreams we used to fill our heads with when we were children. However, our imagination is powerful and vital to our success and happiness. We rarely use it to its full potential in our daily lives, so imagine what we could accomplish if we did use it.

What you think you become. When you concentrate your energy and focus on one thing, you almost attract it to yourself (Mueller, 2016). Every thought and feeling that passes briefly through us saturates itself with energy. The more we focus on a particular thought or idea, the more energy we are putting into it. When we are unhappy in situations that we find ourselves, we tend to focus all our energy on those situations. We will spend hours going over the things we are dissatisfied with, replaying scenarios in our heads. For example, if we are unhappy in a relationship, we will spend our time obsessing and continually thinking about it. We will replay arguments we have had with our partner, or obsess about the little things they do that make us unhappy. We spend so much time and energy focusing on the things making us unhappy that we end up perpetuating them, and nothing ever changes. However, if we were to spend that time instead, by visualizing the things we felt were missing in the relationship, we would find ourselves unconsciously making decisions to see that future. We underestimate how changing our thought patterns change our actions, and therefore change the things we can achieve.

You might be feeling overwhelmed at this point because you think that you might not have the best imagination: many people experience this. They will sit down and start the process of creatively visualizing but grow frustrated and give up when they cannot produce vivid or perfectly detailed scenarios in their head. However, it is something that takes practice. It is not always going to come to you immediately. Furthermore, if you do not quite understand this, you will be stressed when practicing, which will ultimately undermine the process. It will take time to learn how to visualize clearly and with focus.

Furthermore, many people do not think visually, but rather, they think in feelings or using their other senses (Harell, 2018). This does not diminish the effectiveness of their practice—you need to learn what method works best for you. The most important part about visualization is forming vivid, tangible thoughts about the goals you are trying to achieve. Determining whether you are a visual or non-visual thinker is central to this.

Visual Images

To visualize something is to see something in your mind's eye (Harell, 2018). As previously mentioned, for some people, this comes naturally. You can ask them to think about their childhood bedroom, and they can see it clear as day—right down to the small details such as the books they had on the shelves or the color of the carpets. If you can see such clear and vivid pictures in your mind, you are a visual thinker. Being able to conjure up images in our mind is one of the most powerful things our consciousness is capable of doing.

Many people assume that when we speak about creative visualization, our conjuring thoughts are entirely visual. Although creating visual images is essential, that does not necessarily mean that you should only use images when you creatively visualize. Even though your other senses are not as prominent in your thought process, creative visualization becomes more effective when you use them to create a more detailed picture. This is because the more information you give your mind, the easier it is for you to "accept and internalize a new concept" (Kotsos, 2019). By building up your visualization with your other senses—such as associated emotions, smells, and sounds—you create a more rounded and realistic picture. Because these thoughts are more detailed, they feel more realistic; you are, consequently, more likely to succeed.

Lastly, everyone processes information differently. While some people are image-orientated, others are more kinesthetic or auditory-orientated (Gawain, 1995). Let us look at the non-visual images conjured up during creative visualization.

Non-Visual Images

As previously mentioned, not everyone visualizes using imagery. Just as people lean on different senses to learn and interpret the world around them, people also tend to imagine or visualize using different senses (Gawain, 1995). This is evident in the way people store memories;. In contrast, some people catalog their memories visually, other people have distinct memories for different smells or sounds.

We can start by using the example of a father trying to

become more active to be healthier. He might have a mental image of him in the future—fitter, leaner, and being able to run around with his kid in the park because of this. Focusing on this image alone is strong, but using his other senses would strengthen it. Say, for example, he imagined hearing his son's gleeful laughter because his father was running around and playing with him. He could also imagine that he can feel his body's strength and its ability to run and do things he was never able to before. Maybe he can also focus on the smell of the fresh air in the park. Beyond his sense, he can focus on how it makes him feel emotionally to play with his son and feel happy and healthy. Now he can concentrate on his son's happiness, as well.

One could choose any number of these aspects to focus on when visualizing such a future. Perhaps the image feels more realistic to you when you focus on the sounds or the emotions attached. Maybe it feels more realistic if you were to focus partly on the image but mostly on how it would feel physically. Any of these variations of creative visualization are valid. It takes practice: an understanding of your mind works to figure out where on the spectrum you find yourself. The most important thing is that the visualization feels like reality to you.

FOUR

Therapeutic Benefits
_____

THE BENEFITS OF CREATIVE VISUALIZATION IN BOTH PHYSICAL
and emotional realms are almost endless. The design of
creative visualization helps you figure out and work towards
the best version of yourself, in whatever capacity you find you
need improvement. It is about using your imagination to
create the things you want in life (Brenner, 2016). Therefore,
creative visualization's therapeutic benefits are endless and
dependent on what you are trying to achieve. You can
improve your physical health by visualizing exercising and
leading a healthier life. You can improve your mental health
by using creative visualization to heal from past traumas and
minimize the anxiety you associate with it. You will feel more
confident and ready to tackle any obstacle, as long as you
decide that you will.

Improve Health

Creative visualization can massively improve your health
through its abilities to reduce stress in your life. Stress is detri-
mental to your physical health because it impedes the func-

tioning of your immune system. When we are stressed, our body releases the hormone corticosteroid, making your immune system less effective. Our body is unable to fight off infections, and we are more likely to get sick. Stress can also lead to unhealthy coping mechanisms such as drinking or binge eating. It is even more likely to affect the general functioning of all parts of your body (McLeod, 2010).

However, in our current fast-paced world, it almost feels as if it is impossible to avoid. Stress can be particularly harmful when we feel incapable or like we lack purpose or direction. Creative visualization reduces stress, encourages relaxation, builds confidence, and focuses on your goals in life. It helps to get your mind back on track when you feel imbalanced. Preparing you to deal with any high-stress situations—but allowing you to imagine and conquer them beforehand. There are several specific practices for reducing stress using creative visualization. An example practice is where you lie back and envision all the tension in your body like lava. You imagine it leaving your limbs, lower body, and arms—all pooling in your head. You then envision the lava running out of your ears and leaving your body altogether: your muscle loosening, and your whole body relaxing (McNaney, 2015). Exercises like this can help you to physically destress. Combined with the overall calming effect that creative visualization has, it will significantly reduce your stress levels and increase your health.

Creative visualization can also benefit your health as it allows you to work towards a future in which you adopt healthy habits. It is used as a method by many athletes because practicing it can help you maintain a healthy lifestyle through hard times. It does this by allowing you to "mentally prepare for challenging circumstances, you can develop coping strategies and better respond to future anxieties" (McNaney, 2015). It helps you to create a headspace where not only can you achieve healthy habits such as eating better and working out, but you can also maintain them. This is essential for your overall physical health.

Morale Booster

Through creative visualization, you will find yourself achieving things you never thought possible before. It allows you to "mentally create pictures of events that you want to be manifested in your life" (Kollam, 2013). By focusing on what we want and creating ideas of what we are capable of—fully believing them—it massively boosts our confidence and sense of self-belief. Nothing boosts your morale and sense of self-worth more than knowing that

you are capable of achieving your goals. It allows you to focus on all the things your life can and will become a reality, given the right time and effort.

It boosts your morale because you begin to understand that you have more control over the quality of your life and your general happiness than you perhaps previously believed. Nothing leads to low morale and feelings of helplessness more than genuinely believing you have no control over your life and the things that happen to you. You may feel that life determines itself already for you: you are not capable of certain things, so why even try? Creative visualization gives you back control over your future, which is massively motivating and morale-boosting.

Lastly, the act of channeling positive thoughts and rejecting negativity will instantly boost your confidence. We are often not aware of how pessimistic we are on a daily basis and how much repeating negative ideas about ourselves devastates our confidence. If you are continually thinking about how you are not capable of something—refusing to chase your goals because you believe you will fail—all the energy you are putting into that is willing that outcome into existence. However, if you rewire your thinking to believe that you are capable and constantly visualize yourself succeeding, you will start believing it. Your confidence and self-belief will be genuinely high.

Forgetting Fear

One of the biggest obstacles that we face in trying to improve ourselves is fear. We typically become riddled with self-doubt and apprehension; we are afraid that we are not capable, afraid of change, and afraid of failure. Often, we spend so much of our energy focusing on our fear that it causes those fears to manifest, rather than the goals you were going after in the first place. Denning & Phillips (1981) touch on this, stating that "Fear attracts the very things we do not want. Fear is a compelling emotion, and that energy, tied in with an image of the thing feared, creates the very circumstances for the feared thing to happen."

Practicing creative visualization allows us to forget and look past our fears. It is about focusing on the positive and focusing on a reality where your fears do not exist. If you are focusing all your energy on visualizing scenarios, it leaves little space to focus on the fears that would hold you back.

Lastly, creative visualization can help you heal from past traumas that form the root of anxieties you still carry around today (Webster, 2006). By working through and healing those past wounds, you can move forward and be confident without those fears holding you back. While you do not forget the actual event, changing the negative thought patterns surrounding it allows you to lose the emotional attachment you have to the event. You are, therefore, no longer scared of repeating it (Brenner, 2016). It also allows you to associate positive emotions with things that used to cause you anxiety. For example, perhaps the last interview you had went horribly. You embarrassed yourself and did not get the job; now, even another interview concept terrifies you. You would use creative visualization to relive the interview but replace the moment where you messed up with moments where you succeed. You visualize impressing the interviewer and getting the job. By repeating this practice repeatedly, it will dominate the original memory and create confidence within you that will replace the fear.

FIVE

The Key to the Law of Attraction

PERHAPS THE MOST CENTRAL FACTOR OF CREATIVE visualization is the Law of Attraction. The Law of Attraction is a law that governs the universe and states that whatever you put out into the universe, you are bound to attract back to you. It is a force that "guides people's lives and is the underlying power behind all things" (Hooper, 2007). It is present in our everyday lives and always has been, whether or not we take note of it. When we invest emotional energy into anything, we unconsciously call it towards us because "desire is a form of energy" (Denning & Phillips, 1981). This idea is the law of attraction and, more importantly, the basis of why creative visualization is effective.

The Law of Attraction has been around for centuries. In the second century of the Common Era, Marcus Aurelius, the Roman Emperor, said, "Our life is what our thoughts make it" (Hooper 2007). The first time it was labeled the Law of Attraction was by Russian writer Helena Blavatsky in 1877. However, the first person to suggest it as a general principle was Prentice Mulford in 1886. he was a vital figure in the development of the New Thought movement. He discussed the theory of the Law of Attraction at length in his essay

"Law of Success" (Larson, 2017). It is clear from this that though the idea has always been around and present, it has only recently been formalized as a theory.

One of the most common interpretations of the Law of Attraction is attracting either positive or negative forces into our lives. If you are naturally positive, you will attract positive things and positive people into your lives. Similarly, if you focus on the negative parts of life, you will draw that naturally. This is because "whatever we give our attention to becomes our point of attraction. It becomes the thing that we magnetize into our lives" (Hooper, 2007). If you are naturally cynical, this is not something that stays within your thoughts—it affects and colors every part of your life. You are more likely to be unhappy because you cannot see the positive in any situation. Your negative feelings will also inform any decisions you make. If you expect the worst-case scenario from any situation, you will never make decisions that would risk that. You are likely to miss out on the best things that could happen to you because of that thought. Hooper (2007) confirms this, stating that "The negative tendencies that people pursue in their lives often help to confirm the initial fears that they have. They lose their jobs, their friends, and their closest loved ones to problems that seem beyond their control." We are unconsciously making decisions like this every day. So, how do we use the Law of Attraction to our advantage?

Using creative visualization is the key to fully utilizing the Law of Attraction. It is about understanding that every thought you have has meaning and has power. It is recognizing that you see your life as negative because you are putting that negativity out there. For example, if you find yourself thinking that people are always leaving, ask yourself what you are attracting when you meet new friends. Are you starting new friendships envisioning that they are not going to stick around? Are you constantly replaying those negative thoughts and even complaining about them to your friends?

These negative thoughts and behavior patterns are attracting friends to you that will not stay, most likely because of your behavior. However, you can use creative visualization to imagine a future where you have more profound and longer-lasting friendships. By rewiring this, your thoughts towards new people will become more positive. You will automatically attract those people into your life.

Understanding how the Law of Attraction works is vital to understanding why creative visualization works. Your thoughts have energy, they determine your behavior, and they attract similar energies to them. By guiding your thoughts, you can choose what you bring into your life.

SIX

Types of Visualization

WITHIN THE BROAD PRACTICE OF CREATIVE VISUALIZATION, there are several different ways to practice it: the general formula tends to be the same. To practice creative visualization, you would use a free 30 minutes in your day to find a quiet space. Put away your phone, and ignore all other distractions. You need to start with a goal: a future goal you want to manifest, or perhaps a past trauma that you want to move past. You will then sit down, close your eyes, and breathe deeply. Until you feel completely focused and calm. Visualize the scene you are trying to manifest in your head, focusing on the details and making it feel as real as possible. Do this for several minutes and repeat the entire exercise at least once a day.

However, there are different ways to speak to yourself and ways to envision your thoughts. The three main types are receptive visualization, programmed visualization, and guided visualization. Deciding on which type to practice depends entirely on the individual and which method creates the most realistic and effective scenarios for them.

Receptive Visualization

The first type of creative visualization is receptive visualization: this is the most passive form of creative visualization. You are essentially just sitting back, relaxing, and allowing your inner thoughts to stream in. It is quite similar to watching a movie in your mind's eye, except you control the scenes. You begin apart from everything and then slowly allow yourself to be pulled into the action (Gawain, 1995).

As usual, you would start by finding a quiet space and settling into it. Close your eyes and take several deep breaths until you feel calm and centered—then you can begin. Try to picture the scene you want to visualize, allowing the subconscious to fill in blanks and other smaller details that you had not previously imagined. While you are ultimately in control, you do not force anything but instead, sit back and truly listen to what you want. Build up the image in your mind until you feel like you are at the center instead of passively watching. When you feel as if the scene is realistic, you have succeeded.

For example, you could use receptive visualization to visualize getting a new job. You will close your eyes and get into a calm and meditative state. You can start by allowing ideas to slowly come to you, ideas about what you want in a job: for example, the working environment, the type of work, the people, the hours you would work, or perhaps what the office space is like. You will slowly build up an image through all these small ideas that gradually come to your mind. Eventually, you will find yourself immersed in the vision as it starts to feel more and more realistic.

Programmed Visualization

The second type of creative visualization is programmed visualization. It is perhaps the most common form of creative visualization and the more active form. This is when you actively engage with your inner self. Instead of passively waiting for the desired image to fill your mind, you engage in a dialogue with your subconscious mind and create the image together. For example, if you wanted to lose weight, you would start the visualization by actively asking questions about why you want to lose weight. How much you want to lose, and the healthy ways in which you can do it. You will essentially have this conversation with yourself to uncover what you truly want, and this process will build up to a visualization.

Furthermore, a key part of programmed visualization is repeating the same visualization process every day to bring a specific goal or scenario into reality (Webster, 2006). The idea is that you spend at least 30 minutes each day replaying the same exact scenario in your head. There should be a conversation with your inner self every day; however, the general image or scenario should stay mostly the same. For example, if we looked at the previous example of losing weight, you would focus on an image of yourself at a lower weight. Happy, healthy, and able to exercise and be strong. Perhaps you are going for a strenuous hike with friends, and you can keep up without any problem. You would visualize this same scenario every day, possibly adding different details such as which friends are with you or which specific hike would be doing. By continually replying to the same scenario, it starts to feel more and more real until your subconscious accepts it as reality.

Guided Visualization

The last type of creative visualization we will discuss is guided visualization. This involves listening to a taped or spoken script, which leads you through the visualization by asking you to conjure up specific images or inner experiences (Gawain, 1995). This will involve listening to either a tape or recording of someone speaking and guiding you through a visualization practice. You can find a variety of different techniques, depending on what you are looking for with visualization. There are ones that focus on general well-being and happiness, reducing stress, and cultivating a more productive and positive mindset. Others help the listener focus on achieving personal or professional goals that they may be striving for (Martin, 2016).

Guided visualization begins that same way most creative visualization practices do. You would find a quiet space and make yourself comfortable. However, you would then deviate by either listening to the guided mediation through speakers or, more preferably, through headphones. Using headphones helps the listener to focus and become completely immersed. There may be soft music in the background of the visualization. The speaker will speak in a soothing voice. You will be asked to visualize certain things and take along a journey of images (Martin, 2016). Because these guided visualizations are not personalized, the images will often be vague and metaphorical. You will project your own life or current situation onto them to find meaning.

Guided visualizations are particularly useful if you are beginning your journey with creative visualization because it teaches you how to start the process. The person guiding the visualization also often has a soft and soothing voice, which helps get the listener into a calm and meditative state. Guided meditation is suitable for people wishing to make general improvements or those just starting their journey.

SEVEN

Visualization With Other Techniques

VISUALIZATION IS JUST ONE OF MANY MINDFULNESS TECHNIQUES
that can reduce stress and help create a balanced and happy
life. Furthermore, practicing different techniques such as
meditation and hypnosis in conjunction with visualization can
often magnify their effects.

A few of these techniques are relaxation, self-hypnosis,
meditation, and increasing your willpower or mental strength.
Using these other techniques alongside creative visualization
will be incredibly helpful if you are just starting your visualization journey, as they will help you relax, focus, and increase
your mental capabilities and the ability to control your
thoughts.

Relaxation

Relaxation is perhaps one of the most important prerequisites
for creative visualization to work. If you are not entirely at
peace, it is often hard to truly focus on the image that you are
visualizing. Suppose you feel stressed about things, and your
mind is wandering. In that case, the scenarios that you are

visualizing will not feel real when they become lost among a thousand other thoughts. Additionally, anxieties and limiting thoughts are what prevent one from reaching success (Kollam, 2013). The goal of creative visualization is to remove them; however, it is a lot harder to achieve this state if we are not relaxed.

There are multiple ways to practice relaxation—ideally, the practice would begin before you start creatively visualizing. They are used to center you and get rid of negative and intrusive thoughts and emotions. Various methods include deep-breathing techniques, aromatherapy, or using music or meditation.

We will go into more detail about tips on achieving a relaxed state in the next chapter.

Self-Hypnosis

Self-hypnosis is a powerful relaxation technique that can be increasingly effective when used in conjunction with creative visualization. While many people might marvel at the idea of using hypnosis for good. It is, in fact, "a serious therapeutic tool that can help people overcome many psychological, emotional, and even some physical problems" (Cohen, 2010). While the concept sounds intimidating, it is something that happens to us more often than we realize. Any time you have lost yourself in an activity, such as reading a book or watching a movie, completely unaware of how much time has passed, you essentially lulled yourself into hypnosis. These experiences are often spontaneous, and you are unaware of them (Bernhardt & Martin, 1978). However, when utilized to its full potential, the ability to self-hypnotize can be an invaluable skill.

In order to start self-hypnosis, you need to have a strong desire and an open mind (Bernhardt & Martin, 1978). If you are skeptical, it will not work. Hypnosis does not necessarily achieve one specific thing but instead achieves what you want it to. It is goal orientated and serves as a way to focus on desires. Self-hypnosis can help break or form habits or increase confidence and general well-being. Hypnosis puts you in a highly focused and also highly-suggestible state (Cohen, 2010). More importantly, it can be useful in forming a new skill. To enter into self-hypnosis, you have to start much the same way you do when intending to creatively visualize: you will find a quiet space and settle in. Then, you begin breathing deeply and repeating the same silent suggestion to yourself: "My eyes are tired and heavy, and I want to sleep now" (Cohen, 2010). Repeat this over and over again until you feel

yourself falling into a deep state of relaxation. You can continue in this state for several minutes, focusing on your breathing. You can suggest things to yourself, for example, "You are going to succeed through creative visualization." You can also suggest to yourself the goals you are going to achieve. When you are finished, count up from five in a lively manner and slowly become aware of your surroundings once more.

Self-hypnosis can help form the skill of creative visualization and help you enter into a relaxed and calm state that visualization also requires.

Meditation

Practicing meditation—in conjunction with creative visualization—is beneficial not only because it helps you achieve a calm and relaxed state with ease, but also because it allows you to control your mind. Meditation is a space where your body and mind are deeply connected. It frees you from "troublesome and fragmented thoughts, memories, and emotions, so your mind is clear and alert, whole and complete" (Ashokananda, 2015). This is particularly important when practicing creative visualization because it allows you to focus wholly and entirely on what you are trying to visualize.

Specific meditation methods teach you how to focus on allowing negative thoughts that enter your head to drift in and out without focusing on them (Harell, 2018). Honing this skill of ignoring negative and intrusive thoughts that limit you is highly beneficial for creative visualization. It allows you to visualize without intrusive thoughts affecting your practice.

To meditate, you need to find once again a quiet and safe space where you can close your eyes and focus without any interruptions. Start by breathing deeply, completely emptying your mind; to stop your mind wandering, you can focus on counting your breaths. If you do have intrusive thoughts, acknowledge them but do not allow them to stick. Do this for several minutes or for as long as you can focus. Slowly return to breathing normally and open your eyes when you finish.

Meditation is an invaluable skill in learning how to focus and gain full control of your mind. It will aid your practice of creative visualization in many ways.

Your Willpower

Motivation and willpower are essential components to foster to visualize effectively; as previously mentioned, you need to have full control over your mind for creative visualization to work. While this can be achieved with practice, generating mental strength will help you get into an efficient place a lot faster.

Willpower is like any other muscle in the body. Therefore, it needs to be trained and honed until it comes naturally to you (Cummins, 2013). You can build willpower in multiple ways, most notably trying to practice self-control in small ways every day. You can also use imagination and creative visualization to convince yourself of self-control.

Creative visualization is something that requires constant

practice. It should not happen once and then forgotten about: you need to have the willpower to get up and do it each and every day. More importantly, you need the motivation to do it properly and give it your all. Therefore, exercising and improving your willpower is highly beneficial in practicing creative visualization.

EIGHT

Achieving a Relaxed State

As stated multiple times, achieving a relaxed state is essential to a productive visualization. When you are deeply relaxed in your mind and body, it changes your brain waves. Your brain waves become slower and deeper: this is the alpha level, and it shows us a healthy stage of consciousness. There have also been discoveries that show this state of consciousness is a far more effective one to effect change, such as changing habits or beliefs (Gawain, 1995).

One of the easiest ways to achieve a relaxed state is to carefully choose when you practice creative visualization. It is helpful to do it at a time of the day when you are already naturally relaxed and calm, both physically and mentally. For this reason, many people chose to visualize in the evening just before you go to sleep and in the morning right after you wake up (Gawain, 1995). Because you are so close to sleep, your body is naturally relaxed and receptive at these times. However, you need to be careful that you are not so relaxed that you fall asleep. If you are prone to this, instead get out of bed and sit in a comfortable chair to practice. It is also helpful to practice in a chair because "Having your spine straight helps the energy flow and makes it easier to get a deep alpha wave pattern" (Gawain, 1995). Furthermore, you can create a calming and cozier atmosphere in little ways: one method? Dimming the lights.

Outside of the time of day you chose to practice, there are multiple ways in which you can achieve a relaxed state to practice creative visualization. One of the easiest is to practice deep breathing techniques—this is almost a form of meditation. You begin by breathing deeply and slowly, holding in your breath for five seconds, and letting it out slowly for seven seconds. Then, starting from your toes and slowly moving up, relax your body muscle by muscle. Do this slowly and methodically until you feel loose and calm. This is a simple and effective technique; however, if you still find yourself physically stressed, there are additional ways to relax. You can choose to take up mindfulness techniques such as yoga or meditation.

Aromatherapy can also be highly effective in relaxing you —it alters your brain waves. It reduces the stress hormone's presence, 'cortisol,' which allows you to feel relaxed and content (Scott, 2009). Aromatherapy is a more passive way of getting into a relaxed state, as all it requires you to do is either light candles or turn on a diffuser. However, it can be very useful. Particularly if you find the scents that are right and helpful for you in feeling calm and focused. Calming scents to try would be lavender, chamomile, or honeysuckle (Scott, 2009). However, the scent is not always the most important. Some suggestions show the mere ritual of lighting candles. Creating a warm and calm space adds to the relaxation powers of aromatherapy.

You can do any of these methods in combination with one another to reach a relaxed and meditative state that is conducive for visualization. This method will also be dependent on your stress levels from day to day. Some days, you might start off relaxed enough naturally. On other days, you will find you need to use aromatherapy and deep breathing techniques to get into a space where you are comfortable enough to focus on creative visualization. It is dependent on you and what works best for you as an individual.

NINE

Steps for Creative Visualization

NOW THAT WE HAVE FULLY ESTABLISHED WHAT CREATIVE visualization is and the broader concepts that drive it, let us look at the specifics of how you need to start. Creative visualization is mainly about mindset. There are a couple of specific ideas you need to enter the process to succeed.

Passion

To change is something you need to want completely. You need to be passionate about your goals and what you want to achieve. Also, you need to be passionate about the idea that visualization can help you achieve your goals. Creative visualization is dependent on the complete and unwavering belief that what you are envisioning is achievable, and convincing yourself that it is already a reality. None of this would be possible without the passion and a compelling desire to improve your life and your happiness.

Identify

The first step of visualization is to identify what you are trying to change (Mueller, 2016). There is no reason to start if you do not have something you are trying to achieve—you need to sit down and take stock of your life. Look at the different spheres: Are you happy professionally? Are you satisfied with your social life and friends? How about in your relationship? Really take the time to focus on where you think you are lacking. Once you have identified an area where you want to improve, delve into the specifics of what you want.

When you start out, pick goals that are more attainable and easy to believe in (Gawain, 1995). It will allow you to practice visualization without too much initial negative resistance from yourself. When you are more adept, you can tackle bigger and more challenging goals.

Pictures

What would visualize be without pictures? As we previously discussed, not all visualization needs to be entirely visually orientated; whether you are using your other sense or not, being able to mentally picture your goals is essential. You need to see the situation clearly, and it needs to feel completely real to you. Suppose you are struggling to visualize things in the beginning. In that case, you use real pictures by creating a 'treasure map' or 'vision board' for your goals. This idea would be a collage of images and texts representing your goals and what you would like to achieve (Gawain, 1995). This is helpful if you are starting out, and you need something to help you focus and visualize.

Share Your Dreams

To give words to something is to make it real. The temptation to keep our goals and ambitions to ourselves is there. If we tell everyone and we fail, we see that as embarrassing. However, by hiding our goals, we are less likely to achieve them. We need to accept the possibility of failure; otherwise, we will never try, and we will never succeed.

Furthermore, the more we speak about our goals, the more real they feel. The key to creative visualization is that the visualizations need to feel real. Tell all your close family and friends what your goals are and your plans to use creative visualization to achieve them. Not only does this make the goals feel real, but it also holds you accountable to go through with it. Next time Aunt Jenny asks about how your plans to get fit are going, you want to tell her you are progressing.

Commit

As previously mentioned, you must be passionate about what you want and how you will achieve it. In the same breath, it is necessary that you completely commit to your goals and the process of creative visualization.

No to Negative Nancy

Negative and limiting thoughts are the enemy of creative visualization. They impede your ability to believe in yourself and truly see yourself achieving the things you want to happen. Therefore, you must banish all negativity and focus instead on positive thinking.

To attach positive energy to your goals, you can use affirmations. You can make positive statements out loud to yourself, or focus on yourself, achieving the things that you want in life. When you do this, focus mainly on banishing any doubts that may come into your mind (Gawain, 1995). It is also beneficial to recognize the thoughts or ideas you have that have negativity attached to them. Spend time undoing those negative attachments and turn them into positive ones.

Speak It

Speaking things into existence makes them feel more real. As previously mentioned, talking to those around you about your goals is one way to bring your goals and thoughts into reality. Perhaps equally important is saying those same things to yourself.

One way to practice this is to use affirmations. To change your life, you need to change your thought patterns (Sasson, 2001). Affirmations help in this because you are essentially speaking things into existence. If you say something over and over again enough times, you will start to believe it. Use affirmations about achieving your goals and in leading a happier and more fulfilled life. Say them to yourself often and with intent and belief—eventually, you will start to believe them.

Meditate

Meditation encourages mental focus and relaxation, two aspects that are key to visualization. Meditation is an invaluable skill that teaches you how to calm yourself down to the extent that you can focus entirely on something.

Additionally, it also teaches a person how to acknowledge negative thoughts and subsequently banish them (Harell, 2018). These two skills are invaluable for creative visualization. It allows you to focus entirely on what you are trying to visualize and banish any limiting thoughts that would impede your practice. It is almost essential to practice meditation alongside creative visualization.

Believe

Lastly, and perhaps most importantly, you need to believe in what you are doing completely. You need to trust in every aspect of this process. You have to believe in the practice of creative visualization. Believe in your goals, and acknowledge that you are more than capable of achieving them. You need to have faith (Kotsos, 2019). If you cannot see yourself realistically achieving your goal, you are not genuinely practicing creative visualization.

The success of creative visualization is entirely dependent on you, and you need to believe in yourself completely. You are more than capable of achieving anything and everything that you put your mind to.

Conclusion

Creative visualization is an immensely powerful practice that is accessible to everyone. It is first and foremost about believing that you are capable of more. It is about believing that your mind is more powerful than you give it credit for and knowing you can do better and more extraordinary things. It is about knowing that this is not dependent on anything external, but just reliant on you and how hard you try.

The practice of visualization should start out as a mindful activity but ultimately become something you do whenever you make decisions. In the beginning, you should choose specific goals to focus on and set aside time every day to practice visualizing achieving those goals. While you will always carry on this ritual, the act of creating reality from your imagination should leak into every action and choice that you make. Eventually, it will become second nature for you. You will find yourself subconsciously making decisions that lead you to the life you want in every aspect imaginable.

Furthermore, you will always attract what you are putting out into the universe. Simply deciding that you want to improve and that you want to begin practicing creative visualization is the most significant step in attracting improvement and happiness into your life. By deciding that you want to make an active effort to do better and be better, you are already starting to reshape your mindset and rewire your subconscious. In terms of self-improvement, the first step is always the hardest. However, by simply deciding to make a change and take control of your life, you have already started getting through the most challenging part.

The uses of creative visualization are endless—it is a practice that is easily workable to fit your needs and what you are personally trying to achieve. It can help you create a new way of thinking and, subsequently, a whole new way of living. Because you are rewiring some of your basic instincts, it is a method that will take time and a lot of practice. It is not something that will come instantly or naturally but something that takes time and concentrated effort.

Do not give up because it does not come easily. It is important to remember that you are trying to undo years or decades of negative or limiting thought patterns. Just 30 minutes of creative visualization is powerful enough to do years of damage but only when done consistently and well. It will take time to visualize effectively or figure out which method and which spaces work best for you when doing so. Take all the knowledge you have gained here and take the time to learn how to implement creative visualization into your daily life. Not only will it benefit your mental and physical health, but you will also find happiness and confidence that you could never have even dreamed of before.

You are capable of anything you can imagine—you just have to visualize it.

References

Ashokananda, S. (2015). Power of Relaxation: Align your Body, your Mind, and Your Life Through Meditation. Watkins Media Ltd.

Bernhardt, R., & Martin, D. (1978). Self-Mastery Through Self Hypnosis. New American Library.

Brenner, A. (2016). The Benefits of Creative Visualization. Psychology Today. https://www.psychologytoday.com/us/blog/in-flux/201606/the-benefits-creative-visualization

Cohen, M. (2010). How To Use Self-Hypnosis To Achieve Your Goals. Hypnotherapy, Hypnosis, CBT and Counselling in Sutton. https://www.hypnosisandhealing.co.uk/self-help-centre/how-to-use-self-hypnosis-to-achieve-your-goals/

Cummins, D. (2013). How to Boost Your Willpower. Psychology Today. https://www.psychologytoday.com/us/blog/good-thinking/201306/how-boost-your-willpower

Denning & Phillips. (1981). A Practical Guide to Creative Visualisation. Llewellyn Publishing.

Gakkai, S. (2020). The Three Realms of Existence.

Nichiren Buddhism Library. https://www.nichirenli-brary.org/en/dic/Content/T/165

Gawain, S. (1995). Creative Visualization. New World Library.

Harell, T. (2018). What Is Creative Visualization? Better Help. https://www.betterhelp.com/advice/visualiza-tion/what-is-creative-visualization/

Hooper, D. (2007). Law of Attraction: How to Attract Money, Love, and Happiness. Kathode Ray Enterprises.

Kollam, D. P. (2013). Creative Visualization - 4 Guiding Principles to Getting Ahead. Living in Well Being. https://www.livinginwellbeing.org/creative-visualization-4-guiding-principles-to-getting-ahead/

Kotsos, T. (2019). Creative Visualization Explained. Mind Your Reality. https://www.mind-your-reality.com/creative_vi-sualization.html

Larson, C. (2017). Your Forces and How to Use Them. Dover Publications Inc.

Martin, I. (2016, May 17). Guided Visualization: A Way to Relax and Reduce Stress. Psych Central. https://psychcen-tral.com/lib/guided-visualization-a-way-to-relax-reduce-stress-and-more/

McLeod, S. (2010). Stress, Illness and the Immune System. Simply Psychology. https://www.simplypsychology.org/stress-immune.html#:~:text=When%20we

McNaney, J. (2015). 5 Benefits We Can Reap From the Power of Visualization Immediately. HuffPost. https://www.huffpost.com/entry/5-benefits-we-can-reap-fr_b_6672638

Mueller, S. (2016). The Power of Creative Visualization. Planet of Success. http://www.planetofsuccess.-com/blog/2016/power-of-creative-visualization/

Ramsay, K. (2019). The Three Levels of Human Consciousness. Medium. https://medium.com/acholy/the-three-levels-of-human-consciousness-6d9a59fed577

Sasson, R. (2001). Creative Visualization - Attracting Success with Mind Power. Success Consciousness. https://www.successconsciousness.com/blog/creative-visualization/creative-visualization/

Scott, E. (2009). How to Use Aromatherapy for Stress Relief. Verywell Mind. https://www.verywellmind.com/aromatherapy-for-stress-research-and-techniques-3144598

Webster, R. (2006). Creative Visualization for Beginners. Llewellyn Worldwide.

About the Author

Monique Joiner Siedlak is a writer, witch, and warrior on a mission to awaken people to their greatest potential through the power of storytelling infused with mysticism, modern paganism, and new age spirituality. At the young age of 12, she began rigorously studying the fascinating philosophy of Wicca. By the time she was 20, she was self-initiated into the craft, and hasn't looked back ever since. To this day, she has authored over 40 books pertaining to the magick and mysteries of life.

To find out more about Monique Joiner Siedlak artistically, spiritually, and personally, feel free to visit her **official website**.

www.mojosiedlak.com

f facebook.com/mojosiedlak

twitter.com/mojosiedlak

instagram.com/mojosiedlak

pinterest.com/mojosiedlak

BB bookbub.com/authors/monique-joiner-siedlak

Other Books by the Author

African Magic

Hoodoo

Seven African Powers: The Orishas

Cooking For the Orishas

Lucumi: The Ways of Santeria

Voodoo of Louisiana

Practical Magick

Wiccan Basics

Candle Magick

Wiccan Spells

Love Spells

Abundance Spells

Herb Magick

Moon Magick

Creating Your Own Spells

Gypsy Magic

The Yoga Collective

Yoga for Beginners

Yoga for Stress

Yoga for Back Pain

Yoga for Weight Loss

Yoga for Flexibility

Yoga for Advanced Beginners

Yoga for Fitness

Yoga for Runners

Yoga for Energy

Yoga for Your Sex Life

Yoga to Beat Depression and Anxiety

Yoga for Menstruation

Yoga to Detox Your Body

Toga to Tone Your Body

A Natural Beautiful You

Creating Your Own Body Butter

Creating Your Own Body Scrub

Creating Your Own Body Spray

Last Chance
Join My Newsletter!

If you missed it, I have a free gift available for you and wanted to remind you it's still available.

mojosiedlak.com/self-help-and-yoga-newsletter

Thank you for reading my book.
I really appreciate all your feedback and would love to hear what you have to say! Please leave your review at your favorite retailer!

www.ingramcontent.com/pod-product-compliance
Lightning Source LLC
Chambersburg PA
CBHW071637040426
42452CB00009B/1662